D0926206

JOHN MAGEE: THE PILOT POET

JOHN MAGEE

THE PILOT POET

*including all his known works
and a short biography by Stephen Garnett*

JOHN MAGEE: THE PILOT POET

First published 1989 (Hardback)

Second Edition, 1996

Published by This England Books,
Alma House, 73 Rodney Road, Cheltenham,
Gloucestershire, GL50 1HT.   Tel: 01242-577775.

© This England Books 1996

Printed in England by BPC Wheatons Ltd.,
Hennock Road, Exeter, Devon, EX2 BRP.

ISBN 0 906324 22 X (Paperback)

John Magee in the uniform of the Royal Canadian Air Force.

ACKNOWLEDGEMENTS

The publishers would like to thank the following for
their valuable assistance in the preparation of this volume:

The Magee family — Mr. Christopher Magee,
Mr. David Magee and The Reverend F. Hugh Magee;
Dr. A.H. Lankester; Mrs. Elinor Wright;
The Reverend Trevor Hoy;
Mrs. J. Macrory, Librarian of Rugby School;
Mr. Winston G. Ramsey, Editor, *After the Battle*.

Further Reading

Sunward I've Climbed by Herman Hagedorn
(Macmillan, New York, 1942).

Contents

Illustrations

FOREWORD

by Roy Faiers
Editor of This England

Oh! I have slipped the surly bonds of Earth …
… Put out my hand and touched the face of God.

As the American space shuttle "Challenger" roared off into the sky on that fateful day in January 1986, the eyes of the world were upon it. Television cameras zoomed in to capture close-up pictures of what was expected to be yet another triumph in the spectacular programme which had put the United States well ahead of all other nations in the field of space research. The "Challenger" carried a crew of seven astronauts, including two women. A short time before the launch, they had been seen waving and smiling to the crowds gathered at the scene as they boarded their space craft. It seemed almost routine as the commentator's voice calmly took up the countdown and people cheered the lift-off. Then came those dramatic moments, watched by millions of people on television all over the world, when the main rocket exploded and the shuttle itself, with all its laughing crew, disappeared in a billowing plume of white smoke. Time seemed to stand still as the numbing horror ot if all burned into the sight and minds of the helpless witnesses down below.

In his speech to the American people following the disaster, President Reagan quoted a few lines of verse in an effort to lessen the deep sense of shock suffered by his grieving nation and the world at large. The poem he considered most appropriate to soothe the mental wound caused by the tragedy was "High Flight", written on September 3rd, 1941, by a young Spitfire pilot, John Gillespie Magee, the son of an English mother and an American father. Three months after writing the poem on the second anniversary of the outbreak of war, John was killed in a mid-air collision over Lincolnshire. He was just 19.

Following the President's poignant reference to his verse, newspapers throughout the world scrambled to find some details about the virtually unknown poet. In their files they found an article on John Magee which had appeared in *This England* magazine four years earlier, written by Dr. A.H. Lankester, a friend of the Magee family, and containing most of the information they required. Excerpts from that article were widely quoted next day in the Press and *This England* later published a reprint of it for free distribution. Because of the reaction to that article, and the newly-awakened interest in John Magee as a result of the President's reference to his verse, we decided to publish all the known works of the remarkably gifted young man who has been called "The Pilot Poet", together with a more detailed biography of his short but very worthwhile life, researched by a member of our own editorial staff. Since the first edition of this book three more of John Magee's poems have been discovered by his family, and these are now published (pages 125-128) for the first time.

C hina in the first decades of the the 20th century was a country in ferment. Following the revolution of 1911 and the demise of the Manchu dynasty, anarchy and chaos were rife, with that once-great cradle of civilization and culture split into fragments and at the mercy of its feuding generals.

In the middle of all this upheaval, disregarding their own safety and sustained only by the strength of their faith, were a number of Christian missionaries — men and women from every corner of the globe and all sorts of backgrounds who were devoting their lives to spreading the word of God amongst the native population. One of these missionaries was an American named John Gillespie Magee, a remarkable man from a well-to-do Pittsburgh family who had turned his back on a life of wealth, influence and opportunity in Pennsylvania (an uncle was a state senator, a cousin had been Mayor of Pittsburgh for many years) to become a priest of the Episcopal Church and a missionary in China.

He arrived in that vast land of colour and excitement in 1912, a tumultuous time in the wake of the Chinese Revolution, and was soon presiding over a large mission in the bustling city of Nanking. John became a highly respected figure amongst the members of the Christian community and kept an open house for any Chinese who came to him for help and advice. He worked on his own for several years, but when an equally remarkable 28-year-old English lady arrived in Nanking in 1919, so closely-knit were the English-speaking people in the city it was inevitable that the two should eventually meet.

Faith Emmeline Backhouse was the daughter of the Rector of Helmingham in Suffolk, a peaceful out-of-the-way spot which could hardly have been more different from the noisy rickshaw-crowded streets of Nanking. But just as John Magee had chosen a different life from that which had been expected of him, so she too had looked for something more than the quiet existence offered by a typical English village.

Before becoming ordained, Faith's father had led an exciting life on the high seas, travelling round the world twice before he was in his 'teens and eventually becoming second mate on board a sailing ship. It was from him that Faith inherited her adventurous spirit, as well as the religious fervour that she possessed from a very early age. Faith went to China as a member of the Church Missionary Society — a daring and highly unconventional step for a young English lady in those days, but once she had learnt the language it wasn't long before she was working hard alongside John Magee in Nanking. After overcoming some initial opposition from Faith's father, an Englishman of very firm views who was rather perturbed that his daughter should have chosen an American, the couple were married at Kuling on 19th July, 1921.

The first of their four sons, also christened John Gillespie Magee and the boy who would one day write that soaring anthem to flyers everywhere, "High Flight", was born on 9th June, 1922, at Shanghai. He would be followed by David Backhouse (6th July, 1925), Christopher Walford (19th August, 1928) and Frederick Hugh (23rd August, 1933).

Faith and John were both very proud of their origins and keen that their sons should also have knowledge of their Anglo-American roots. They planned, therefore, when the boys were old enough, to send them first to school in England and then to college in America. Before that, John started his education at the

American School in Nanking, speaking English while he was there and then reverting to the Chinese tongue when he returned to the mission compound in the evening. Fighting frequently broke out close to the city and Faith often had to take the young boys to Shanghai for safety.

John was at the school in Nanking for three years until November 1931. Then when he was nine, as the first part of his "English" education, he was sent to St. Clare's boarding school near Walmer in Kent. Mr. Magee stayed behind in China, but John was accompanied on the voyage by his mother and two younger brothers. Faith Magee's father had died some two years earlier and so she was anxious to spend more time with her mother than her husband's leave would allow. The journey was long and tiring, but very exciting. They sailed from Shanghai on the P & O liner *Naldera* via Colombo and the Suez Canal to Marseilles in France. There they disembarked and travelled by train to Paris and then on to Calais. Once at the French port they started the last stage of their journey by Channel steamer to Dover, which they reached on 5th December. Within a few hours they had at last reached their final destination — "Foxburrow", Grandmother Backhouse's cliff-top home at Kingsdown in Kent, which enjoyed spectacular views of the Straits of Dover. The house, so close to the legendary White Cliffs — those powerful symbols of England for people the world over — must have seemed ideal to Faith as a starting point for introducing John to his English origins.

Mr. Magee visited his family in England during the following summer. In the meantime, John had started at St. Clare's where he was soon demonstrating exceptional intelligence and an adventurous spirit. His

teachers were conscious of "a soaring mind always aiming at the stars". He excelled at classics, learnt to play the piano in just one term, but with confidence and experience unusual for one so young rebelled against the tedium of routine and was always quick to instigate or join in with any mischief. It was during his

△*Some present-day pupils of Rugby School enjoy a game of cricket, just as John Magee did when he was a boarder there.*

last year at St. Clare's that John started writing poetry. In 1935 when he was 13 his parents moved him to Rugby's famous public school in Warwickshire — an institution steeped in English history which as well as

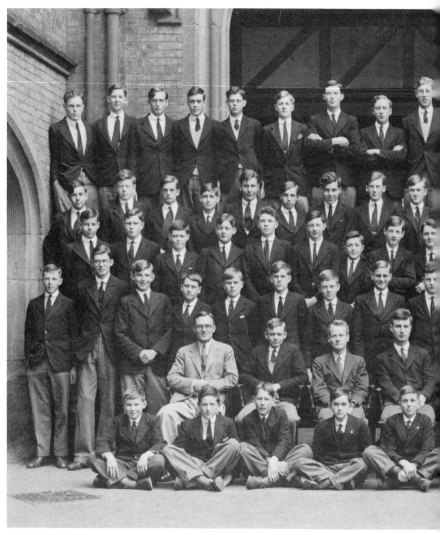

△The boys of School House photographed with the headmaster P.H.B. Lyon in 1936. John Magee is sitting in the front row, fifth from the left.

being at the centre of England geographically was also at the heart of her culture and traditions. Life for boys at the school was based on a strict hierarchical structure revolving around daily services in the chapel, the

well-ordered house system and the frequently cruel custom of "fagging" which was still in operation in English public schools.

Nevertheless, for all the emphasis that was placed on discipline and service to the school as a whole, there were still great opportunities for individuals to emerge

△One of Rugby's most esteemed Old Boys, the First World War poet Rupert
Brooke (1887-1915), with whom John Magee felt a particularly close affinity.

from the crowd and shine. From his very first day at Rugby, John would have been keenly aware of the boys and masters who had passed through the school before him and gone on to leave their mark on England and the wider world. His unusual background compared with most of the other boys, his greater experience of the world and his sharp, questioning mind, marked him out as something of a rebel, a free spirit who was unwilling to be fettered by the rules and regulations that his more conventionally brought up contemporaries tended to take for granted.

Trevor Hoy, John's room-mate at Rugby from 1935 to 1939 with whom he shared a tiny closet-like study, remembers him as "an audacious rule-breaker and pioneer" following in the footsteps, in many respects, of William Webb Ellis who is commemorated on a plaque in the school's famous Close. He it was who, in 1823, "with a fine disregard for the rules of football as played in his time, first took the ball in his arms and ran with it, thus originating the distinctive feature of the Rugby game".

All of the boys at Rugby were well acquainted with the story of William Webb Ellis and these words on his memorial. During the 1930s, as war clouds gathered over Europe once again, they also became increasingly aware of the 600-plus former students of the school who had fallen in the First World War and whose names were recorded in the school chapel.

To John Magee, one name on the tragic roll of honour stood out with particular meaning and poignancy — that of the celebrated war poet Rupert Brooke (1887-1915) whose work he greatly admired. John's own attempts at writing verse were arousing favourable comment amongst his teachers, and the headmaster, P.H.B. (Hugh) Lyon, who was himself a gifted poet

△Hugh Lyon, Headmaster of Rugby from 1931 until 1948.

RUPERT BROOKE
1887-1915

IF I SHOULD DIE THINK ONLY THIS OF ME:
THAT THERE'S SOME CORNER OF A FOREIGN FIELD
THAT IS FOREVER ENGLAND. THERE SHALL BE
IN THAT RICH EARTH A RICHER DUST CONCEALED;
A DUST WHOM ENGLAND BORE, SHAPED, MADE AWARE
GAVE ONCE HER FLOWERS TO LOVE, HER WAYS TO ROAM,
A BODY OF ENGLAND'S, BREATHING ENGLISH AIR,
WASHED BY THE RIVERS, BLEST BY SUNS OF HOME.
AND THINK, THIS HEART, ALL EVIL SHED AWAY,
A PULSE IN THE ETERNAL MIND, NO LESS   GIVEN;
GIVES SOMEWHERE BACK THE THOUGHTS BY ENGLAND
HER SIGHTS & SOUNDS, DREAMS HAPPY AS HER DAY;
AND LAUGHTER, LEARNT OF FRIENDS; & GENTLENESS,
IN HEARTS AT PEACE, UNDER AN ENGLISH HEAVEN.

with several published books of verse to his credit, took the boy under his wing.

"Some day," Lyon said to him, "you are going to write much better poetry than I am writing."

Hugh Lyon had been headmaster at Rugby since 1931 and would remain so until 1948. He had a profound influence on John Magee, his own early life giving him a special sympathy with boys like John whose parents were frequently abroad. Born in 1893 at Darjeeling, India, where his father was a member of the Civil Service, Hugh had also been sent to England to

△John Magee (on the right of the picture) during a holiday in the Lake District with the Lyon family, April 1937. Elinor Lyon, the headmaster's eldest daughter who became a special friend of John, is in the centre of the group.

be educated — first to a preparatory school and then to Rugby. He went up to Oxford in 1911 but joined the army in 1914, serving with the Durham Light Infantry. In 1917 he was awarded the Military Cross and then, after being wounded, spent the last few months of the war in a German prison camp in Poland. His collection of poems *Songs of Youth and War* was published in 1917, and when he returned to Oxford after the war he won the prestigious Newdigate Prize for poetry. His other publications included *Turn Fortune* (1923) and *The Discovery of Poetry* (1930), as well as several hymns. He also wrote the popular comic song "The Company Sergeant Major".

The quality of the following poem in which he

recalled his friends who had fallen in the trenches made his words to John Magee about writing "much better poetry" all the more noteworthy:

These were my friends — ah stay and tell again
Those lovely names! The grave voice passes on;
That lantern searching through the field of dead
Lights one by one the sleepers, and is gone.

Yet not at once the darkness covers them;
Then only falls the night, when men forget.
O careless friends, O passionate swift eyes,
Dear friends who loved me, you are with me yet,

You are names now; but not as other names,
That live an instant when the man is dead
In old folks' thoughts, or crumble with the years
Chiselled on stone above the muffled head:

Coming unshaken by the years, your feet
Still eager on the track, those eyes alight,
With tales upon your lips, as children tell
The rich hours over ere they say goodnight.

You perish not! When we and ours are swept
Unnumbered waves upon the one dark tide,
Sons of our sons shall keep this festival,
And praise and ponder on the men who died.

In 1920 Hugh Lyon married Nan Richardson and for five years from 1921 he taught at Cheltenham College. He was made Rector of Edinburgh Academy in 1926, and then returned to Rugby, his old school, in 1931.

John Magee became a close friend of the Lyon family (there were three daughters, and a son who was to die tragically young in 1943, aged only 14) and was one of several schoolboys who accompanied them on picnics and holidays in Yorkshire and the Lake District. They were tremendously happy occasions — especially for John who saw very little of his own family — and full of laughter and much childish horseplay. At this time John developed a deep, adolescent affection for Elinor, the headmaster's eldest daughter, who was a year older than himself. During a short holiday at Robin Hood's Bay on the Yorkshire coast he wrote the following poem for her:

> *If, when we walked together in the rain,*
> *While tears and raindrops mingled in our eyes;*
> *And talked of foolish things, to ease the pain*
> *Of parting; when we thought we could disguise*
> *Our feelings in the light of stolen joy;*
> *When fawning bracken kissed our sodden shoes,*
> *And hand in hand, determined to enjoy*
> *Those last few moments we were soon to lose,*
> *We walked in silence, awed by shrouding mist*
> *And wondered at that silent wilderness*
> *Of moor and mountain, and the pall above,*
> *And laughed awhile — and sometimes all but kissed;*
> *If then we found a little happiness,*
> *Did neither of us see that this was . . . Love?*

John was convinced that he was in love with Elinor, although she (being a year older and the daughter of the Headmaster) while liking John, tended to think he was rather young and she was anxious not to encourage him too much. On one occasion while at Rugby, John asked Elinor if she would play tennis with him on

△*Robin Hood's Bay on the Yorkshire coast. John spent a romantic few days there.*

the school courts. She politely refused. A short time later she received a small packet containing a razor blade and this scribbled note from her disappointed suitor: "Why don't you come and do it properly?"

The young poet was well and truly smitten and he continued to idealise Elinor right up to the end of his short life.

Described by his housemaster as "intelligent, volatile, emotional, untidy, thoughtless, keen", John enjoyed life to the full at Rugby, playing football and tennis, taking part in rifle-practice, and during the holidays sailing his own dinghy on the Channel. Hugh Lyon had been President of the Oxford University Dramatic Society and he continued to produce plays at Rugby, with John Magee among the actors.

John did well in his studies but was still inclined to throw himself into wild pranks, like the time he climbed onto the roof of the School House and tied a label with his name on it to the hand of the clock. The boys sat in small cubby-holes to study and John's was always the one from which the most giggling and chattering came.

As news filtered over to England from Europe, and the possibility of another war loomed larger and larger, they were difficult times for the boys, uncertain as to what their futures should be. Having been through it himself once before, Hugh Lyon recognised this but was keen to stress that, whatever happened, the values that were being taught at Rugby would be just as important in the future. At the school speech day in 1938, John and all of his fellows heard their Headmaster communicating this belief with powerful eloquence:

"Whatever may come of our present discontents, whether the storm breaks or floats away, there will be need in the world ten or twenty years hence of fresh efforts by a new generation to build on a surer basis. It is for that fresh start that we should educate our children now. We of our generation have made our effort and it looks like being a gigantic failure. Yet we have struck one or two good blows, and they have brought into concrete form the idea of world co-operation. And if everywhere else in the world man must of necessity be concerned with salvage work with makeshift devices, with making friends with the mammon of unrighteousness, with balancing peace against injustice, war against dishonour, surely we in our schools must be busy with work which, even if less urgent, is more fundamental. The eternal ideals remain: truth, love, justice, sympathy, and loyalty. They do not perish because men are false to them. They will return again when we have again become worthy to entertain them. This is to be the responsibility of the next generation. Such energies as we have must go to their education for this finest of all vocations."

On one memorable holiday in 1939 John was invited by Professor C. Franklin Angus, Vice-Master of Trinity Hall, Cambridge, whom he had recently met, to join a reading-group of Cambridge undergraduates at Mortehoe, a quiet village on the beautiful North Devon coast. The members of the group would read together in the mornings and then spend the afternoons tramping around the countryside or along the golden expanse of Woolacombe sands. Being in such strong intellectual company stimulated John immensely and he became firm friends with a young South African of their number called Geoffrey Sergeant. The two of them spent many hours discussing every subject under the sun, sharing their deepest aspirations and ideas as they had never done before. That John could feel so at ease among these sharp-minded students was a tribute to his own intelligence and learning. Sergeant wrote a glowing tribute about the young Magee:

"He became and remains the most lovable and the most inspiring of my friends, the companion with whom above all I wished to face the difficult tasks of the future".

John was a boy who would never accept anything without first questioning it, and having grown up just after what was supposed to have been "the war to end all wars", and with first-hand experience of warfare from his childhood in China, in the uncertain atmosphere of 1939 his thoughts turned towards pacifism and doubts about conventional religion which was so important at Rugby and in his parents' world. This frame of mind was revealed in his poem "Brave New World" which he completed during that idyllic spring-time holiday at Mortehoe. The 10-verse poem was intended, in John's own words, "to portray, with the assistance of Three Voices (supposed to represent Disillusionment, the voices of the Dead, and a chorus of Angels) the Aspirations, Disillusionment and subsequent Re-encouragement of a central figure I have called Youth".

It was with this poem that John won the coveted Rugby Poetry Prize in 1939. His hero, Rupert Brooke, on whose work he based many of his own creations, had won the same school prize in 1905. John even wrote his own "Sonnet to Rupert Brooke":

We laid him in a cool and shadowed grove
One evening, in the dreamy scent of time,
Where leaves were green, and whispered high above
— A grave as humble as it was sublime;
There, dreaming in the fading deeps of light —
The hands that thrilled to touch a woman's hair;
Brown eyes, that loved the Day, and looked on Night,
A soul that found at last its answered prayer . . .

△Sixteen-year-old John showing his mother the letter informing him that he has won the school's Poetry Prize.

There daylight, as a dust, slips through the trees,
And drifting, gilds the fern about his grave —
Where even now, perhaps, the evening breeze
Steals shyly past the tomb of him who gave
New sight to blinded eyes; who sometimes wept —
A short time dearly loved; and after, — slept.

After the exciting interlude in Devon when John had found himself listened to and taken seriously by men with much more mature minds than his school-mates, he returned to Rugby restless and dissatisfied. Hugh Lyon, with his great understanding of adolescent boys and their problems, urged John to be more tolerant and less self-opinionated, but the aspiring poet was growing up fast, his moods fluctuating between exultation and depression. He was also still in love with Elinor.

Despite being one of the brightest boys, John's schoolwork declined and he started to question all the rules and conventions of public school life. This emotional turmoil spilled over into holidays at "Foxburrow", where his mother and brothers were now living while Mr. Magee remained in China. He felt uncomfortable and out of place, but was always honest about the reasons and full of remorse for the disruption that he caused. He poured out his feelings in letters to his mother:

"I know I'm simply frightful at times, but I don't really mean to be. I know I tend to live for my own enjoyment, but I think I'm being quite truthful that I don't do this just for the sake of enjoyment itself. It's just like drugging myself. I find life frightfully depressing at times and I simply have to get my thoughts away into the skies. That's why I suddenly rush off at unearthly hours to the cinema, to the sea, up on the Downs with my gun, to see a friend. I have to find an outlet for my emotions. When I get like that, I just haven't the power to be nice to anyone; I immediately retire into my shell, put out my bristles, and shun the company of men . . ."

So, long before he ever climbed into the cockpit of an aeroplane and "slipped the surly bonds of earth", John was already desperate to slip the bonds of boredom and anything that made life predictable and a numbing routine.

John's communications were frequently forwarded to his father who, being himself in the middle of a war which would have disastrous consequences for China if Japan were to be victorious, was at pains to temper his son's commitment to pacifism. He replied to John wisely and patiently that certain things could come about which were even worse than war. John was impressed with his father's arguments, but he remained convinced that war was ultimately futile, and uneasy about the possibilities of a forthcoming conflict.

In the summer of 1939, so that he could complete his education and also get to know something of his American roots, John was persuaded, rather against his wishes, to go to America and stay with his aunt in Pittsburgh, Pennsylvania. He travelled third-class on the *Queen Mary*, befriending a group of pretty young girls and falling in love with one or other of them at regular intervals. He was welcomed with great enthusiasm by his relatives, and his aunt arranged for him to have guest privileges at an exclusive and expensive country club which provided him with riding, polo, hunting and fishing, followed by convivial evenings with plenty to drink until the early hours.

Of course, with his zest for life and unflagging energy, John entered into the social round of parties and dances with wild abandon, but unfortunately he spent far too much money and his aunt and uncle were horrified at the unpaid bills that started to arrive. Part of the trouble was that John was terribly homesick, even more so when war broke out in Europe and his beloved England, with all its intense memories of people and places, came under threat. He felt cut off from his friends and pestered the American State Department to give him a passport, but to no avail. After he failed in an attempt to get a job in Pittsburgh, his family decided that the present situation could not go on and he was found a place further east at the Avon School near Hartford, Connecticut.

Avon was an outstanding school and the plan was for John to follow the Magee family tradition and go on to Yale where his father had graduated. It was also in a lovely, picturesque setting, but because of his unusual background and the depth of his experiences compared to those of his schoolmates he found it difficult to settle down and make friends. One of the masters at Avon recalled the occasion when he invited John and several other boys round to his rooms for tea:

"John, with his aura of sophistication and charm, was rather like a cockatoo in a cage full of pigeons. He looked at everything — pictures, books, furniture, and the other young men — with an unabashed interest. It was apparent at once that he was sensitive, intelligent, and perhaps even a little priggish. We fell almost at once into a discussion of modern poetry, with the pigeons flapping rather feebly behind . . ."

Although described by one of his teachers as "the most intelligent person who has ever come to the school", John still rebelled against the school system and also became disillusioned with the way of life he had come across in America. This was a very narrow experience on which to judge, but because of his continued homesickness and longing for England, he tended to magnify any faults that he found. He wrote to Hugh Lyon about it and almost cried out with frustration:

"I shall never be really happy over here. Don't you believe a man should live by his convictions? I am convinced my place is in England and, if ever I see the opportunity, I'm coming."

Thanks to the encouragement from Lyon, who urged him to "stick it out", and the friendship he enjoyed with a group of like-minded souls who shared his enthusiasm for discussion and debate, life at Avon did improve for John. His Mayfair accent, ability to read classics with ease, and continuing dare-devilry, certainly singled him out as someone very different from his fellows. He was intolerant and highly critical of most of them, preferring to seek out the company of the masters with whom he could talk about everything from girls and poetry to philosophy and religion. He borrowed their books, often reading beneath the bedclothes until two or three o'clock in the morning.

Every minute of his spare time was filled with some activity or other. He visited various relatives, dated a constantly changing stream of pretty girls and, most importantly, got to work in the school printing shop and produced an attractive little volume containing 17 of his poems. Copies were circulated privately to his family and close friends, but it was never made available to the public.

△*It was 1940 and the bombs were falling on London. John longed to be involved in the war so that he could help prevent scenes of devastation like this.*

John wrote a Foreword to the book, stating with modesty that it had been produced "not as being in any sense a work of art, but rather as a potential object of interest for those of sufficient curiosity to read it". All he asked was that the poems be read "not too critically, and that they be permitted by the Muses to give some pleasure to my contemporaries, but more particularly to those for whom Youth is but a laughing ghost of the Long Ago".

This deft use of words, which the poems went on to demonstrate even more emphatically, showed what a remarkable 17-year-old John Magee was.

Despite the satisfaction that seeing his poems in print undoubtedly brought him, by the spring of 1940 John was becoming increasingly restless. Like all civilised people he still deplored war, but it was impossible to stand back and watch with indifference as Hitler's rantings grew more and more shrill and his greedy armies gobbled up Denmark, Norway, Belgium and Holland, and were streaming into France. The newspapers were also full of the incredible evacuation from Dunkirk, when 340,000 British and French troops were snatched to safety by a rag-bag armada of naval vessels, merchant ships, tugs, barges, and small yachts crewed by their owners. Not only did John find it impossible to concentrate on anything else when Great Britain was in such peril, but he was scared that his enthusiasm and creativity, his ability to experience and feel, were dying within him. He felt too safe and comfortable and needed a challenge so that he could prove himself.

John was visited at Hartford by Trevor Hoy, his old American room-mate from Rugby. They discussed the situation intensely, both frustrated at US isolationism and, saddened by news of other schoolfriends who had been killed in the conflict, anxious to get involved and do something themselves.

John announced that he would join the RAF, but when he applied for the necessary visa the American State Department refused to issue it, saying he was too young. John poured out his feelings in a letter to his friend Geoffrey Sergeant:

"At times I think I am going mad with yearning — the vain and insistent groping to be back in the past, when the wind blew in my face from the Channel, and all was ecstacy! Meanwhile England must remain a dream, and I must go on pretending to myself that I am happy here."

On 9th June 1940, his eighteenth birthday, John could temporarily put these worries to the back of his mind with the arrival of his father from China, and his mother, together with the three younger Magees, from England. It was a wonderful reunion, even though John had half longed for it and half dreaded it because of the changes he felt he had undergone during their separation — like his questioning of religion and his free-wheeling independence. But he need not have worried and a very happy time with them followed. Eager to be one of the family again, John took them on holiday to the island of Martha's Vineyard, off the coast of Massachusetts, in a large second-hand car. Even so, Mr. and Mrs. Magee were rather shocked by their son's constant comings and goings: his love for dances, beach parties and reckless drives around the coast. When his bewildered father suggested that perhaps he should try and slow down a bit, John explained the reason for his gallivanting with typical bluntness and candour: "My generation does not expect to live long, and we want to enjoy ourselves while we may".

The only clouds in the sky of what would otherwise have been an idyllic summer for John, were the frequent news reports from across the Atlantic. Following the fall of France, Great Britain, battered but defiant, stood alone, her men, women and children bearing the full brunt of Hitler's anger and frustration as the Führer used his bombers to try and raze their towns and cities to the ground and smash them into submission. Although Mr. and Mrs. Magee were hoping that John would go to Yale in the autumn, as the Battle of Britain raged throughout the summer of 1940 and outsiders watched with breathless admiration the heroism and self-sacrifice of the valiant British and Commonwealth airmen, despite the fact that he had won the top classical scholarship, John's determination to join up became irresistible. After many

This certifies that

_____ John Gillespie Magee Jr. _____

has been admitted to the Freshman Class

entering Yale University in 1940.

_____ Edward S. Noyes _____
Chairman of the Board of Admissions

New Haven, Connecticut _____ July 17, _____ 1940.

The Class will meet for organization in Woolsey Hall, Saturday, September 21, 1940, *at* 10.00 *A.M., daylight saving time.*

△ The entrance certificate to Yale which John was destined never to take up. It was mentioned at the time that John's marks in the Classics entrance examination were the highest in the University's history.

preoccupied days and restless nights, he decided that he could do nothing else but stay true to his feelings.

"I just can't go to Yale," he announced, "I've never felt so deeply about anything before and I have got to get into this and join the Royal Canadian Air Force".

After a long discussion between John, his father and the president of Yale, it was finally decided to let John have his way.

In September 1940, the family were together in New York. On the final Sunday evening before John was due to leave for Canada, Mr. Magee told his son that there was no reason why he had to spend his last night with them, and that they would quite understand if he wanted to go out and have a good time. John, struck by the importance of that final evening, would not hear of it.

"I want to be with you," he insisted, "and I would like to go to church and go away in that atmosphere".

And so they all went to church together, separating the next morning with a mixture of tears and smiles — John pleased that he was at last setting out to do what he felt he must, his parents naturally worried about him but also extremely proud that he had stuck to his principles and chosen such a brave course of action.

All did not go according to plan, however. At his medical in Ottawa John, much to his chagrin, was rejected for being 16lbs underweight and told to return in two weeks to try again. During that time he gorged himself on whatever food he could find, and by assiduously avoiding all exercise eventually managed to reach the required weight and was accepted as Aircraftman, 2nd grade.

John, his head filled with visions of daring deeds in the skies, found life in the Royal Canadian Air Force rather less glamorous to begin with. He was sent to the

Manning Depot at Toronto, where he slept in a large hall with 1,500 men in two-tier bunks, and then to Trenton where he was put on security guard and subjected to strict military discipline. On one occasion, as a result of returning late from leave, he even spent a few days in jail.

Life was tough at Trenton and John filled any spare moments he had by writing long letters home to family and friends. In these he characteristically poured out all his feelings, philosophising in his usual manner and longing for the time when his training would be over and he could soar above the fields and hills of England, defending the country that he missed so much. The possibility of death was often in his thoughts: "I want to die," he wrote to one of his brothers, "in circumstances violently heroic". Mundane though his actual existence seemed in comparison with the prospect of what might eventually come, John was still caught up in the excitement of learning to fly.

"The whole place," he said in another letter, "thrills to the vivid, eager living of men who realize that they are almost certainly in their last year of life . . . An aeroplane is to us not a weapon of war, but a flash of silver slanting the skies; the hum of a deep-voiced motor; a feeling of dizziness; it is speed and ecstasy."

This could be no other voice than that of the poet who would shortly write "High Flight".

Christmas 1940 brought a short spell of home leave in Washington, where Mr. Magee was now the assistant rector of St. John's Episcopal Church in Lafayette Square, opposite the White House, which generations of Presidents had visited for worship. All the family were deeply impressed with what Air Force discipline had done to John. Gone was the irresponsible, rather self-centred boy; in his place, an assured, purposeful young man with a delightful sense of humour and, now, wearing a neat moustache.

The high point of the visit as far as Mr. and Mrs. Magee were concerned came on Christmas Day when they all attended morning service and John said that he should like to stay for Communion — the first time in two years. It was a moving moment for Mr. Magee when he gave his son the Sacrament.

At the beginning of the New Year, John was at the Elementary Flying School in St. Catharine's, Ontario, where he made his first solo flight after just six hours of instruction when the average was 10 or 11. But with his natural high spirits he took unnecessary risks and was very nearly killed when, against instructions, he put his machine into a spin from 6,000 feet and only managed to pull out of it at the last minute. He passed the test to become a Leading Aircraftman, and then learned aerobatics. At the end of March 1941 he was posted to the Service Flying School at Uplands, Ontario, where all his dreams seemed to come true at once, flying the more exciting "Yale" and "Harvard" aircraft.

"I have found my place in the sun," John wrote enthusiastically to a former teacher. "I am finding that flying has been in my blood all the time and I didn't know it".

In one eventful week, however, everything seemed to go wrong. He got lost on a flight, ran out of petrol and was compelled to make a forced landing. Then, shortly afterwards, he misjudged a night landing and demolished his machine. He was punished by a restriction of privileges and made to spend two hours a day washing aircraft.

The dare-devil of Rugby Public School was still

very much alive inside the smart uniform of the aspiring pilot. But it was frustration and impatience more than anything else that led him into such escapades. He was desperate to get to England and become involved in the action; frightened in case the outcome of the war should be decided before he had had a chance to do his bit. Among the bright and lively company of other flyers he was in his element, fired with energy and idealism. His greatest fear, and that of all the other young men around him, was that the glorious chance to become a fighter pilot might suddenly be snatched away from him, by failure, as a punishment for recklessness, or even, perhaps, by some arbitrary decision from on high which might order him to train instead for a place in a bomber crew. At last the time came for him to take his crucial "Wings Test" which he passed as second in his class. It was a proud day in June 1941 when he received that all-important emblem of success from his Group-Captain.

There followed a period of leave with his parents and brothers who had rented a house in Washington. No longer restless and unsettled, John was now happy and full of confidence, although he was still rather troubled as to whether a Christian can ever be justified in hating his enemy.

"I'm afraid if I don't hate him," he concluded, "that his bullets will get me before mine get him".

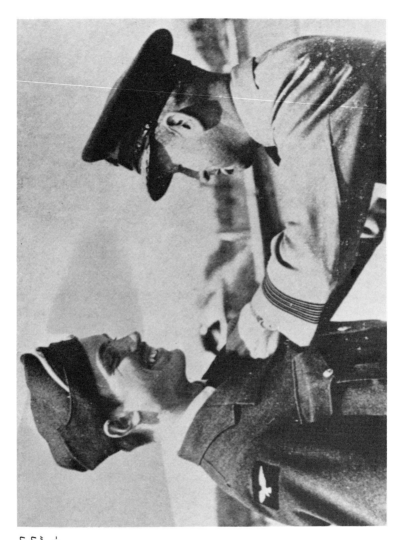

△ The red-letter day in June 1941 when John received his "Wings" from his Station Commander.

50

It was a joyful time, almost as if John had never been away from the family. There was always plenty of noise and activity when John was around, even more so on this occasion as David, Christopher and Hugh had friends dropping in and out of the house at all hours. John took the family into the countryside for picnics and wrestled good-naturedly with his brothers just as he had always done — sticking up for Hugh, the youngest, in any squabbles or horse-play. But everyone noticed how John's life in the Air Force had wrought certain changes in him. The discipline and companionship of other brave men had made him more mature, with a new-found humility and an awareness of his own limitations.

One morning, towards the end of his leave, John was having breakfast when the door-bell rang and the maid handed him a telegram. He read it and then let out a yell that "frightened the pigeons off the roof". The impossible had happened — he had been gazetted as Pilot Officer.

John went to Montreal to get fitted for his new uniform — and much to his delight was saluted for the first time by an army corporal! After a slow journey across the Atlantic he was at long last back in England, enduring a 24-hour journey in a wartime train — so crowded that he slept curled up in a luggage rack — and spending a week in a "magnificent hotel" before proceeding to his final training station at Llandow in South Wales.

He took the next day off and flew to visit Elinor and the Lyon family in Gloucestershire where they were staying with friends for the fruit-picking season. John terrified the sleepy little village as he buzzed low over the house before landing in a field. It was a dramatic and memorable return after two years.

△*A spring day at Kemerton in Worcestershire. John treated the sleepy village to a spectacular aerial display.* W.R. BAWDEN

"It was a joy to see him again," wrote his Rugby headmaster, "he was on top of the world. All the poet-adventurer in him found outlet and expression in the Air Force."

Although he had courted and apparently fallen in love with many other girls during his stay in America (even, on occasions, announcing that he was engaged to be married), it was Elinor for whom John had always kept a special flame burning in his heart. Just as being away from England had led him to idealise the country and its great traditions — especially its literary traditions — so the absence had encouraged him to think of Elinor in heightened, romantic terms. She, on the other hand, though extremely fond of this mercurial, impulsive, well-meaning and totally honest character, did not think of their relationship in quite the same way and tried to discourage him without hurting his feelings. Nevertheless, when he visited her again after giving an impressive display of aerobatics above the heads of the startled villagers, she did notice, as they walked together on Bredon Hill one evening, how much more self confident and improved in manners he was — even if, under his dashing RCAF moustache and self-consciously smoked pipe (which he soon discarded) he still seemed to be very, very young.

John enjoyed life at the training camp, taking to the air whenever he could and staying up for as long as possible. Flying was a close second to poetry as his greatest love and one of the supreme moments of his life was his first flight in a Spitfire on 7th August 1941.

In 1941 it was the ambition of every young man to be a Spitfire pilot. During the Battle of Britain, in the hands of Allied airmen whose courage and endurance astonished the world, it had proved itself to be the swiftest and most deadly fighter plane in the skies. Once a pilot had experienced the Spitfire's unique qualities of speed and manoeuvrability he remained loyal to it for the rest of his life, and even ordinary men and women who were never likely to get anywhere near its snug-fitting cockpit, kept a special place in their hearts for this scourge of the German Luftwaffe. The low, steady sound of its engine in the skies overhead became as familiar as birdsong; its sudden appearance, flashing like an arrow across the blue sky, a tremendous comfort and a potent symbol of freedom in Britain's darkest hours. Men who had flown the

△*A Spitfire patrols the Northumberland coastline in July 1940.*

Spitfire waxed lyrical about its superb aerial performance and awesome fire-power, saying that it came closer than any other craft to embodying the ease and grace of the birds themselves.

John Magee was no less fulsome in his praise. "It is a thrilling and at the same time a terrifying aircraft," he

wrote, "it takes off so quickly that before you have recovered you are sitting pretty at 5,000 feet". It was while he was in the mess one day at Llandow, talking in a loud, excited voice about the qualities of the Spitfire, that a fellow flyer suggested to him that, as he was interested in writing poetry, he ought to put his feelings down in words. Immediately John took an envelope from his pocket and in no time at all he had scribbled down the words of what was to become the most famous flying poem in the world:

HIGH FLIGHT

Oh! I have slipped the surly bonds of Earth
And danced the skies on laughter-silvered wings;
Sunward I've climbed, and joined the tumbling mirth
Of sun-split clouds — and done a hundred things
You have not dreamed of — wheeled and soared and
*   swung*
High in the sunlit silence. Hov'ring there,
I've chased the shouting wind along, and flung
My eager craft through footless halls of air. . .
Up, up the long, delirious burning blue
I've topped the wind-swept heights with easy grace,
Where never lark, or even eagle flew —
And, while with silent, lifting mind I've trod
The high untrespassed sanctity of space,
Put out my hand and touched the face of God.

Soon after, when he had completed his final training and joined 412 Squadron at RAF Digby in Lincoln-shire, John sent a copy of the verse to his parents with a brief explanation of the poem's genesis: "It started at 30,000 feet, and was finished soon after I landed. I thought it might interest you."

When John had been exiled in America and Canada his one great dream had been to join the RCAF and get to Britain. Now that he had successfully achieved that objective and was undergoing fighter training, he itched to take part in some real action, anxious to know how he would cope, but eager to give a good account of himself. Until this became possible, further spectacular aerial visits to the Lyon family and other friends served to take at least some of the edge off his frustration. On one occasion he managed to obtain a Spitfire without any squadron markings on it and the Lyons were again treated to a display of aerobatics above their house. He then flew off to similarly entertain an old school pal and completed his journey with some low flying around his grandmother's house in Devon, when he inadvertently scraped the top of a bramble bush and left a piece of the aircraft's fabric there!

It was in September 1941 that John joined the all-Canadian 412 Squadron at Wellingore (a satellite of RAF Digby), having received a glowing assessment report from his squadron commander at Llandow which included the passage: "Shows patches of brilliance. Tendency to over-confidence".

Time was divided between practising manoeuvres, taking part in usually uneventful coastal patrols, attacking shipping or intercepting bombers over the North Sea and Holland, and enduring that bane of all fighter pilots during the last war, the nail-biting wait for a call to action, when the shout of "Scramble!" suddenly crackled from the loudspeaker. There were also, of course, the parties in the mess that followed any particularly dangerous or successful exercise. On these occasions John and the other young flyers would unwind and celebrate as only fighter pilots knew how. John was a very popular member of the squadron and there was a great sense of comradeship amongst all of them.

When a rather ancient reconditioned aircraft needed testing, it was typical of John Magee to volunteer for the job. Everything went well until it came to the landing and he was unable to release the undercarriage.

△Pilot Officer John Magee (third from left, third row standing) and the other members of his Operational Training Unit at Llandow, South Wales, 1941.

Only by a series of steep dives did he manage to shake it loose and make a safe landing. To his astonishment he was greeted on the ground by the Station Commander accompanied by the visiting Duke of Kent who had watched the whole action. The Duke complimented John with the words, "Nice work". He was overjoyed.

At the end of October on seven days' leave he visited Oxford where Elinor was now a student at Lady Margaret Hall. John was quite sure that he was in love with Elinor ("She has really turned out to be the most inspiring girl," he wrote, "I enjoy her company more now than ever before . . . Really, I think she must be the girl for me.") Although reluctant to make any plans

for the future, John was keen to complete his education at either Oxford or Cambridge after the war.

Next he went to see his grandmother in Devon and walked to Morte Point, hoping to write some poetry in the place that had meant so much to him and his friend Geoffrey Sergeant. But he was haunted by Elinor and the words just would not come. The gulls seemed to John to be crying her name, and "her face was everywhere". On his way back to Wellingore he called on her again. Elinor, who now lives on the coast of Wales, vividly remembered the meeting:

"Before he went back to the squadron he came to say goodbye and brought an old motor-bicycle he had acquired. It was just like him, I thought, to buy a cycle that kept breaking down and had to be pushed most of the time, and it caused him great

△Elinor Lyon. She joined the WRNS in 1942.

△An airfield comes under enemy attack and fighter pilots dash to their aircraft. In 1941 such sudden calls to action were familiar occurrences at air bases all over England.

amusement by its eccentricities. We shook hands rather solemnly when he went and it seemed rather foolish and inadequate to wish him good luck, because whatever happened he considered himself marvellously lucky and I never remember him complaining of anything. The motor-bike, however, cheered us up a bit; it went five yards and then stopped dead, and when at last it went on again we laughed and John waved his hand and disappeared round the corner."

She never saw him again.

On 8th November, 1941, John was in the thick of the most serious action he had yet experienced and the squadron suffered its first losses. "The 109s," he wrote, "came down in swarms out of the sun. I was terrified at first but, after a while, felt a bit better and had a squirt at one, but another was firing at me so I didn't see whether I hit him or not."

He sent his family another poem, "Per Ardua" (the motto of the Royal Canadian Air Force is *Per Ardua Ad Astra*), and wrote the following dedication and verses:

> To those who gave their lives to England during the Battle of Britain and left such a shining example to us who follow, these lines are dedicated.

PER ARDUA

They that have climbed the white mists of the morning;
They that have soared, before the world's awake,
To herald up their foemen to them, scorning
The thin dawn's rest their weary folk might take;

Some that have left other mouths to tell the story
Of high, blue battle, — quite young limbs that bled;
How they had thundered up the clouds to glory
Or fallen to an English field stained red;

Because my faltering feet would fail I find them
Laughing beside me, steadying the hand
That seeks their deadly courage — yet behind them
The cold light dies in that once brilliant land . . .

Do these, who help the quickened pulse run slowly,
Whose stern remembered image cools the brow —
Till the far dawn of Victory know only
Night's darkness, and Valhalla's silence now?

It was to be the last poem he wrote.

In spite of the danger to which it exposed him and the constant nagging strain it put him under — especially during those long periods of waiting around

which he tried to fill by reading or making model aircraft — John loved the life of a fighter pilot. He
relished the company of the other young men, even
though any friendships were often cut tragically short.
A letter he wrote to a friend revealed how thoughts
about his own possible fate were never far from his
mind . . .

"The squadron contains a hell of a good bunch
of fellows. Our mess at the moment is an old
country cottage in a village about five miles from
the aerodrome — the sort of place where you
bump your head everywhere you go. I have never
had such fun in my life. Frankly, however, I do
not expect to last. It's not a very sensible thing to
talk about on the whole, but to be good you've
got to take chances and you can't win all the time.
Anyway, I'd rather be good. The ordinary world
seems a long way away and unbearably dull and I
can't say that I have a lot of ambition to go back to
it under the same circumstances . . . "

John's flying ability improved all the time and he
was soon a section leader, taking part in operations
over occupied Europe. Although he did not see Elinor
again he kept in touch with the Lyon family and on a
brief period of leave returned to Rugby to visit his old
headmaster. Hugh Lyon, who had played such an
important part in encouraging John to write poetry,
poignantly remembered the young pilot's leavetaking:

"He arrived late one night and, just before he
went back the next afternoon, he came and talked
a little to me as I was sawing wood in my garage.
It was good of him to come round, for he was in
a hurry. He spoke a little about my family, a little
about the prospects of going abroad, but not

PER ARDUA

(To those who listed to England during the Battle of Britain and left such a shining example to us the following verses lines are dedicated.)

(Italics)

They that have climbed the white mists
They that have soared, before the mists awake,
To herald of their ... to them scaring
The thin dawns red ... away folk might take;

Some that left other mornings to tell the story
of high blue battle - quick young limbs that bled;
How they had hundreds of the deeds to glory

" " : field

Because my faltering feet would fail I find them
laughing beside me, steady the hand
That seeks their deadly courage —
                                        yet behind them
The cold light dies in that once brilliant land . . .

To others, who half the quickened pulse run slowly,
Whose stern remembered image coolz the boow —
Till the far dawn of Victory know only
Night's darkness, and Valhalla's silence now?

(P.S. If anyone should want this verse see that
it is accurately copied, capitalised, and punctuated. -)

J.S.h.
R.A.F.
1941

△John in RCAF uniform.

much about anything. It wasn't necessary somehow. 'So in all love we parted.' After he had gone, I went on sawing, and thinking of him, and the fine man he was growing up to be."

A few days later, on 11th December 1941, John was once more at the controls of a Spitfire, the aircraft he loved, soaring high in the sky above the flat fenland countryside of south Lincolnshire. It was a routine patrol, and as John put the plane through its paces he was able to experience as vividly as ever the unique joy of flight that he had so eloquently translated into words and which never left him.

Suddenly, at a moment when he was least expecting it, the deadly fear that had always stalked him struck like a mighty hammer blow. Flying through a bank of cloud he collided with another aircraft on a training flight from the nearby RAF College at Cranwell. Although the circumstances surrounding the crash were not clear at the time, it was revealed later that a farmer in a field near the village of Roxholm witnessed the incident and actually saw John climb out of his doomed craft in an attempt to use his parachute. In the event, it got tangled up and failed to open, so both young men were killed.

It was a tragic accident and not at all the end that John might have wished — in a daring duel with an equally courageous enemy.

He was just 19.

The Station Commanding Officer wrote to John's parents in America:

"I would like to express the great sympathy I and all members of 412 Squadron feel with you in the loss of your son. John was a very popular member of our squadron which, as well as being an operational unit, is also a compact family of its own, and can ill afford to lose so valued a member as your son. He was held in very high regard both as a fighter pilot and a good friend of all with whom he came in contact. His and your unselfish sacrifice in the cause of humanity is a source of admiration and gratitude from all his comrades in the Royal Air Force."

John was buried in the village cemetery at Scopwick in Lincolnshire, close to where he died and alongside the graves of some of his friends who had also been killed. The headstone of his grave bears the first and last lines of his poem "High Flight".

At the time of John's death his masterpiece was virtually unknown, but as John was one of the first casualties of the Second World War to come from a Washington family (the United States had only just entered the conflict, on 7th December 1941), reporters flocked to the Magee home to get the story. Mr. Magee gave them copies of the church magazine in which "High Flight" had been printed. As a result, the next day the poem and a story about John were in newspapers right across America, when it captured the imagination of thousands of people. Before very long "High Flight" had also appeared in a number of British newspapers and during the next few years was included in several collections of poetry.

"When my wife and I saw how deeply he felt about the situation in September 1940, we gave our consent and blessing to him as he left to enter the RCAF. We felt as deeply as he did and were proud of his determination and spirit. We knew that such news might come. When his sonnet reached us we felt then that it had a message for American youth but did not know how to get it before them. Now his death has emblazoned it across the entire country. We are thinking that this may have been a greater contribution than anything he may have done in the way of fighting, for surely our American youth must enter this conflict in the spirit of idealism and faith. May we thank the RCAF for all the training and help

PILOT OFFICER
J.C. MAGEE
PILOT
ROYAL CANADIAN AIR FORCE
11TH DECEMBER 1941 AGE 19

"OH I HAVE SLIPPED
THE SURLY BONDS OF EARTH
PUT OUT MY HAND
AND TOUCHED THE FACE OF GOD"

△*John Magee's grave in Scopwick village cemetery.*   IAN HARVEY

69

you gave our boy. We saw a tremendous change in him when he returned to us from his training, a change that was all for the good. We do not regret that we gave our consent to his going and will forever be proud of him".

John's death came as a great shock to Elinor who first learned about it in a newspaper she was reading. It influenced her to join up and shortly after she became a Wren. Although John had discussed the possibility of studying at Oxford himself after the war, or perhaps getting a job as a flying instructor, he very rarely thought about the future, preferring to live for the immediate moment.

"He liked to live life at full speed," wrote Elinor, "and danger only made life more thrilling. I don't think he could have borne to grow old."

Thinking about the bright boy who had been his pupil as well as a dear family friend, Hugh Lyon voiced sentiments similar to those of his daughter:

"The glimpses he gave in his talk and in his poetry of the restless, questioning spirit which lay behind both his religious awareness and his occasional escapades, always gave promise of that wise maturity which was never to be his. But somehow I couldn't ever think of him as mature; he had the flash of youth as something inherent in him, the swift adventurous response to any challenge, which I hated to think might ever die down into the steady lukewarm glow of middle age."

And from across the Atlantic came some wise words from Paul Child, an art teacher at Avon in whom John had often confided:

"I feel certain that, if there had been more time

△ The site of RAF Wellingore as it looks today. Most of the buildings have been demolished and there are few reminders of its important wartime rôle.

in his life, he would gradually have coalesced the disparate elements which made the complicated, but as yet uncrystallized, person we knew. The tortuous swinging of the religious pendulum and the wild struggle of the aesthetic sensibilities against the prison walls of facts and figures, would have reached a more stable and productive rhythm from which some splendid masterpiece might have emerged."

All were convinced that had John lived longer a great deal more poetry would certainly have come from him. "Brave New World", the poem with which he won the Rugby Poetry Prize, and all the other pieces he wrote between the ages of 13 and 16, were remarkable coming from someone of such tender years.

Then, of course, there is "High Flight" . . . the lyrical masterpiece that put into words, as no other poem

RHILL

UISEN
DREY
REY
HAN
SOUR
BLES
TUE
SEY-
RALD
CENT
CKER

LKER
AKE
FORD
FORD
KER
KER
KER
KER
LACE
RD
RLOW
ERS
SON
SON
MAN
TMAN

J.S.L.WELCH
A.R.WELSH
G.H.WHEATCROFT
R.D.WHEATCROFT
J.A.P.WHINNEY
F.WHITAKER
C.B.WHITEFOORD
R.W.L.WHITTALL
R.H.WHITTING
W.E.WIGGINS
K.H.WILLARD
H.C.WILLIAMS
V.F.WILLIAMS
S.D.WILMOT
H.S.WILSON
T.W.WILSON
V.S.WING
FITZH.WINTLE
D.K.WOLLEY-DOD
L.J.WOOD
S.WORTHINGTON
K.C.G.WRAY
W.R.F.WYLEY

E.T.YOUNG

H.R.EES
H.F.M
H.O.C

The Sword I give

△The Book of Remembrance at Rugby School with (opposite) a close-up of the right-hand page showing John Magee's name.

72

MACLAREN. Robert hillhouse.
Born 2nd March 1898. Son of J.F. Maclaren. Cotton House 1912-15. Colonel. Royal Engineers. M.C. 1918. O.B.E. Accidentally killed 20th May 1941.

MAGEE. John Gillespie.
Born 9th June 1922. Son of Rev. J.G. Magee. School House, 1936-39. Pilot Officer, Royal Canadian Air Force. Killed in flying accident 11th December, 1941.

MALLALIEU. Geoffrey Norman Anthony William.
Born 9th August 1918. Son of Lt. Colonel William Mallalieu, (O.B) Tudor House 1932-34. Major. Somerset Light Infantry. Killed in action. 20th February 1945.

MANSERGH. Geoffrey Ernest.
Born 31st January 1893. Son of E.L. Mansergh. Cotton House 1906-10. Brigadier, Commands s. Staff (late Royal Corps of Signals) M.C. 1916. Killed by enemy action. 2nd June 1940.

MARRACK. Phillip Roland.
Born 19th March 1916. Son of P.E. Marrack. Kilbracken 1930-35. Major. Royal Artillery. Died 26th March 1944

MARS. Peter Richard Campbell.
Born 31st October 1921. Son of P.C.G. Mars. Whitelaw House. 1935-40. Pilot Officer, Royal Air Force. Killed in flying accident. 19th October 1942.

△Trevor Hoy, John's friend and room-mate at Rugby, today. He went on to join the American Church and remembers John Magee as "an audacious rule-breaker and pioneer, a brilliant scholar whose poem High Flight summed up his own short life".

has, the tremendous exhilaration of flying with all its surging freedom and breathtaking beauty. Trevor Hoy, John's room-mate at Rugby, whose own brother was killed in a similar wartime flying accident, thinks that the poem — and especially its opening line — also summed up John's life, for he was always try-ing to "slip the surly bonds" of rigid regulation and convention that would, if they could, drag him down and shackle him to a life of soul-destroying sameness and mediocrity. "High Flight", with its soaring rhythm, is a glorious celebration of a life which is much more exciting, free and vital.

This poem has become the anthem for flyers everywhere and hangs on office and squadron walls throughout the Air Forces of England, Canada and the United States. It has been recited on the radio by celebrities such as Orson Welles; broadcast by the BBC on Battle of Britain Sunday when there is a fly past over London; and was also the inspiration for a painting by C.R.W. Nevinson entitled "The Battlefields of Britain" which was presented by Winston Churchill to the Air Ministry in 1942.

Recently, as was stated in the Foreword, "High Flight" was quoted by President Reagan in the wake of the space shuttle tragedy in January 1986. Awareness and appreciation of the poem have spread far and wide and it is now regarded as a classic piece of war poetry, standing alongside famous works by such major writers as Rupert Brooke, John's literary hero, and inspiring all who recognise the need of the human spirit to strive for greater things. It was a truth learnt by John Magee at an early age, and one that was driving him on with the same rapture and determination on that December day nearly 50 years ago when he clambered into the cockpit, danced through the heavens for the very last time, and really did touch the face of God.

The Poetic Works
of John Magee

The Pilot Poet

HIGH FLIGHT

Oh! I have slipped the surly bonds of Earth
And danced the skies on laughter-silvered wings;
Sunward I've climbed, and joined the tumbling mirth
Of sun-split clouds — and done a hundred things
You have not dreamed of — wheeled and soared and swung
High in the sunlit silence. Hov'ring there,
I've chased the shouting wind along, and flung
My eager craft through footless halls of air. . .
Up, up the long, delirious burning blue
I've topped the wind-swept heights with easy grace,
Where never lark, or even eagle flew —
And, while with silent, lifting mind I've trod
The high untrespassed sanctity of space,
Put out my hand and touched the face of God.

PER ARDUA

(To those who gave their lives to England during the Battle of Britain and left such a shining example to us who follow, these lines are dedicated.)

They that have climbed the white mists of the morning;
They that have soared, before the world's awake,
To herald up their foemen to them, scorning
The thin dawn's rest their weary folk might take;

Some that have left other mouths to tell the story
Of high, blue battle, — quite young limbs that bled;
How they had thundered up the clouds to glory
Or fallen to an English field stained red;

Because my faltering feet would fail I find them
Laughing beside me, steadying the hand
That seeks their deadly courage — yet behind them
The cold light dies in that once brilliant land . . .

Do these, who help the quickened pulse run slowly,
Whose stern remembered image cools the brow —
Till the far dawn of Victory know only
Night's darkness, and Valhalla's silence now?

The poems that follow, from "Lines written on a Sleepless Night" to "A Prayer", were contained in the printed booklet produced by John Magee at the Avon School, United States of America, in 1939 when he was just 17. The book was never made available to the public and the poems are published here for the very first time. John also wrote a short Foreword to the book setting out the reasons for his endeavour. This is reproduced on the facing page.

FOREWORD

This little book is thrust upon the world, not as being in any sense a work of art, but rather as a potential object of interest for those of sufficient curiosity to read it; and the sole reason for the publication of these immature verses is that they may possibly be acceptable to the more indulgent as representing various emotional conflicts occurring in the life of a boy between the ages of thirteen and sixteen, and that they may, perhaps, bring back to the reader, if readers there be, something of his or her own youth, when Wonder was fighting for life in the teeth of Pride, and Love lay shivering under the howling winds of adolescent Cynicism. The fact that I printed them myself, with the invaluable help and advice of Mr. Max Stein, will, I hope, be no great impediment to their acceptability. However, all I ask is that they be read not too critically, and that they be permitted by the Muses to give some pleasure to my contemporaries, but more particularly to those for whom Youth is but a laughing ghost of the Long Ago . . .

J.G.M

LINES
WRITTEN ON A SLEEPLESS NIGHT

I LOVE the moon's soft mist-encircled light;
It weaves a silver spell; the very leaves
Seem turned to silver-stone! — surely tonight
There's something strange abroad! Beneath the eaves
Thrushes are nestling, — hushed; and these I love;
And, too, I love thin spires of smoke, that rise
Like incense to the stars; and then, to move
When all the world's asleep, or to surprise
A wakeful mouse from some close hiding place . . .
I love to think I hear an angel's voice
Hung on the whisper of the wind. This place,
This night, this hour, this sky, are all my choice!
I love the earth, the sea, the heaven above,
But, more than these, the right to say *I love!*

SONNET AFTER CATULLUS:

Vivamus, mea Lesbia, atque amemus . . .

S WEETHEART, to live a life of careless love,
Unharried by the vapidness of Age!
— To live, whether there's sun or moon above
Content, within a lover's tutelage;
To share the dreams of every tranquil night;
Ask nothing more than someone to adore;
So while we live, let kisses bring delight —
Kiss me a thousand times, — a hundred more,
Again a thousand; may we never tire
Of showing outward signs of inward Love
To cool the burning flame of our desire!
And then, lest any envier reprove,
We'll start again, no matter what the score,
— And lip to lip we'll kiss for evermore!

SONG OF THE DEAD
A Reproach to this Century

ALSO our lives were tragic; we believed
In the earth, heavy beneath us, trusted the sun
As it played on leaves and flowers, and we conceived
Truth, and True Beauty, — End of Things Begun;
We, too, have laughed, and sung our hundred songs
The sons we bore were perfect in our eyes
We called them Brave, Original, and Wise;
We saw them slain, with faith we bore our wrongs
Watched we the clouds, — and did not understand
— Longed, too, for happiness; and knew despair,
Lay with our dreams in the gutters, and were deceived
By eyes of women; whispered hand in hand —
And loved the moonlight on a lover's hair —
We were but a day in Eternity, — yet we believed . . .

SONNET TO RUPERT BROOKE

WE LAID him in a cool and shadowed grove
One evening, in the dreamy scent of time,
Where leaves were green, and whispered high above
— A grave as humble as it was sublime;
There, dreaming in the fading deeps of light —
The hands that thrilled to touch a woman's hair;
Brown eyes, that loved the Day, and looked on Night,
A soul that found at last its answered prayer . . .

There daylight, as a dust, slips through the trees,
And drifting, gilds the fern about his grave —
Where even now, perhaps, the evening breeze
Steals shyly past the tomb of him who gave
New sight to blinded eyes; who sometimes wept —
A short time dearly loved; and after, — slept.

SONNET

Si bene quid de te merui, fuit aut tibi quicquam
Dulce meum . . .

I F, WHEN we walked together in the rain,
While tears and raindrops mingled in our eyes;
And talked of foolish things, to ease the pain
Of parting; when we thought we could disguise
Our feelings in the light of stolen joy;
When fawning bracken kissed our sodden shoes,
And hand in hand, determined to enjoy
Those last few moments we were soon to lose,
We walked in silence, awed by shrouding mist
And wondered at that silent wilderness
Of moor and mountain, and the pall above,
And laughed awhile, — and sometimes all but kissed;
If then we found a little happiness,
Did neither of us see that this was — Love?

FANTASY

I THINK, if God had heard my foolish prayer,
And you had loved me as I hoped you would;
And I'd looked up one day, and seen you there,
— And you had smiled, as if you understood
Those dreams that I had always feared profane,
And did not mind; — and if I had but found
The quiet touch of your hand, to keep me sane
When all the long, familiar faces frowned . . .

Then, on some cool and secret-shadowed night
I'd wake, and find in your remembered eyes
The strange new Truth I'd longed to realize —
As when some ploughman strikes a precious stone,
And holding it intensely in his hand
With sudden sweetness knows it for his own.

MORTALITY

WHO can forget white lilies in the spring,
 The agony of poppies, stabbing corn?
— Do you remember once when I was king,
And you my queen, how on the perfect lawn
We ruled the daisies while we laughed at play?
. . . And I must live, to see the colours start
To life; when all the world is young in May,
And honeysuckle rushes to the heart . . .

I will not die, while roses laugh in June,
When Beauty wanders through slow, secret ways,
And sombre winter leaps again to mirth . . .
Oh! Death comes swift and cold, and all too soon —
And I must live, while sleepy summer days,
And You — and You — are lovely on the earth!

IMMORTALITY

I WILL not say that men will not forget you,
Nor boast that your brown eyes will never fade;
I should be living, had I never met you,
But I'd have lived alone, and in the shade . . .
I will not praise your laugh, your graceful walking,
Nor say that death will never close your eyes —
There have been those who praised a woman's talking
— Said it would live for ever. These were lies.

The time will come, dear heart, when suddenly laughter
Dies on the lips, glad hair turns quickly grey;
And *friends* will have forgotten shortly after —
But I shall say, that once your skin was fair,
And as you stood beside me in the trees
A petal fluttered down upon your hair . . .

FRAGMENT:

O.T.C.

WE 'MARCHED' at noon, with laughter
In Chevrolets, and Fords,
With powder-caps for bullets,
And swagger-sticks for swords.

P.B.I.

They marched at dawn, in silence,
And fell before sunrise;
With rotten flesh for faces,
— And cavities for eyes...

THE CYNIC
(With apologies to Rupert Brooke)

THESE I have loathed:
Asthmatic engines; stations;
Tea in the parlour; coughing congregations;
— And coal-scuttles; and coal; and clammy hands;
And business men; and military bands;
Tomatoes; hypocrites, and smelly places,
And ill-concealed emotion; vulgar faces;
Orderly picnics; pavement-written scandal;
And Liverpool; — and cups without a handle;
The adhesive kiss of lipstick; school; and blackboards
(And all that's written on them;) — ugly discords
Struck by aspiring pianists; pyjamas,
When I have lost the cord; and spying farmers;
Meals missed; and ink; the obstinate embrace
Of cobwebs; and my brother's blatant face;

Unripe bananas; — little more when ripe —
And close-cropped hair; wet hands I cannot wipe;
Names unpronounceable; and bowler hats;
My nose, and mutilated books; and spats;
And raucous horns; effluvium of fish;
Plucked eyebrows; mud; to "close my eyes and wish"
For vague delights; tobacco-reeking fingers;
And *pukkah sahibs*; and buses; female singers;
And feet; and stocks-and-shares; and millionaires,
And wealth; but more than all ill-gotten pelf,
I hate my gross, inevitable self.

BRAVE NEW WORLD

O H! I would sing of drinks, and drugs,
Of china lavatory plugs,
Phantasmagoric *jitterbugs*,
— And quantities of smoke!

Of saxophonists with catarrh,
And trumpets tintinnabular
Wailing a last discordant bar
To while away the Blues;

Or shall I sing of Perspiration,
Glandular Coagulation,
The dreaded grip of Night-Starvation,
— Of Dandruff, or B.O.?

For women now have treacly eyes,
Take trouble to de-alkalize,
And tell the most fantastic lies
To obviate their Age . . .

Oh! Brave New World, what proof have we
That all the things that tarnish thee
Will definitely *never* be
   Continued in the Next?

MOMENT FORGOTTEN
(With acknowledgments to A.M.)

T HAT was in the woods, among the heather
Green, green evening in the depth of trees —
And you would not forget this day together
And even if you died there would be these

Moments remembered —
                              and you would return
Some day to me as in a raptured dream
To find the place we loved in, where the fern
Was cool, and kissed the ripples of a stream . . .

*   *   *   *   *

I think, dear heart, there will not always be
Rememberings afterward —
                              for you and I
Had little hope that we could then foresee —
Strange stars are sometimes born into the sky . . .

102

RETROSPECT

G LAD eyes, that laugh to me across the years,
Have you forgotten that November's day
When I beheld you through a mist of tears
White, as a petal blown through skies of grey . . .
Then we were happy, wandered hand in hand
Through life; when all we had was Love, and Youth;
Till you had gone, I did not understand
That your gay eyes were Loveliness, and Truth.

Always there will be loves that drift, as ours;
Beautiful faces, touched by fresher winds
Change suddenly; — and soon are blown away;
Passion forgets her few, ecstatic hours
Soon after, in new hearts, and other minds,
— And finds enchantment for another day!

PROSPECT

I KNOW, dear heart, that some day I shall find you
Alone, and in the evening shade of trees;
Twilight, and hills, and quietness behind you
— A scent I shall remember in the breeze . . .

Always you come, a precious ghost, to haunt
The days, the nights; — in sudden, waking dreams
I find your face; you smile, you beckon; — flaunt
Your lovely self before my eyes; it seems

To love is pain! But did you really care?
Have you forgotten? — Is it all in vain
To breathe out sonnets to the midnight air,
— To long to touch your hands, your lips again?

And yet, I know that some day I shall find you
Alone, and in the evening shade of trees;
Twilight, and hills, and quietness behind you
— A scent I shall remember in the breeze . . .

A PRAYER

SOME evening, when I'm sitting out alone
Watching, perhaps, a cloud across the sky,
I'll feel as if a strange cool wind has blown,
— And suddenly I'll know that I'm to die;

Then I'll remember how we stood together,
And laughed, and kissed the lovely sun to bed;
And how we talked of Death among the heather,
And wondered gaily at the Ancient Dead . . .

When breath comes short, and tears come all in vain,
And in the silence I must realize
That I shall never laugh, nor love again,
May I find, leaning over me, — your eyes.

It was with the following poem and accompanying "Author's Note" that John Magee won the highly esteemed Rugby Poetry Prize in 1939, an award that was especially dear to him as his own literary hero, Rupert Brooke, had won the same school prize some 34 years earlier. When John wrote "Brave New World" he was still only 16 . . .

BRAVE NEW WORLD

Author's Note:

May I be permitted to point out that this is not intended in any way to be a dramatic work, but that the accepted dramatic technique of introducing words as from the mouths of characters has proved most convenient for the purpose of this poem? It is intended to portray, with the assistance of three Voices, supposed to to represent Disillusionment; the Voices of the Dead; and a chorus of Angels, — the Aspirations, Disillusionment, and subsequent Re-encouragement, of a central figure I have called "Youth".

BRAVE NEW WORLD

"A sad and great evil is the expectation of death
And there are also the inane expenses of the funeral
Let us therefore cease from pitying the dead
For after death there comes no other calamity." — (Palladas)

What Agony of Beauty! — How the sad
Long look of moonlight troubles all this place!
A crazy sweetness fills my head, until
The mind is swamped with fullness of the soul . . .
How will this beauty, at the time of death
Come sweeping back, come flooding over me!
How will this quiet hour in after years
Engulf the mind that once beheld its form!
What more could man desire?
                                        — Quiet, and Peace,
You I would have flow over me like water
As some cool wave upon a sun-dried sand —
Here is a soothing rest for the troubled mind
In evening's coolness, fingers of the wind . . .
For here, in this freshening hour of breeze and night-birds
Here is the source of our constant sanity
We who spend years in offices and cars
Who though the slaves of Time can yet sustain
The balance of our twisted nerves and notions
As a heated lover —
                          hearing the song of a bird
Is still, — hears too, perhaps, though undefined
The haunting drift of death in the sombre wind . . .
How many generations loved this place,
And, passing, left to us this privilege?

So we who have come, continuing in their stead
Inherit the spirit and phrase of ancient sagas
Hearing, perhaps, in the whisperings of leaves
Tales that our fathers told when they were here
Feeling, perhaps, at evening in this place
Loves of the morning that our fathers knew
Here where the valley is filled with voices and pine-winds . . .

FIRST VOICE

Soon, soon you too will pass the way they trod
When the sweet air goes bitter at the mouth
When cold birds mourn the leaf that falls from the twig
Then Life goes out, leaving no power to hold him
All men go out at the End as the flowing of water
Carries the leaves down —
                                        none remember it
For even then the time of Youth will be taken
The dogs will bark at evening by his tomb
The moaning curlews wheeling over it
Then in the time of death and evening's strangeness —

SECOND VOICE

The time of Youth is but as a sun that sails
Behind the clouds of time —
                                        or a flickering light
That leaves the earth as soon as it has shone
And memory dims with the coming of age and greyness —

THIRD VOICE

Yes, and the time will come
When you will shuffle with the leaden feet
Of Age the shallow fallen leaves before you
And you will not understand why suddenly sweetness

Fills in the heart of you — nor why the tears
Spring into your eyes, for you will not remember . . .
And you will say Where and When did I know such happiness
But you will not remember —
You will feel the freshening wind on your throat
And it will tug excitedly at your shirtsleeves —
And you will sweat in the effort to recall as one
Who reads a book at night
                  — by candle-light —
And stares
At the black print until the page is blurred . . .

FIRST VOICE

    There will be little enough to forget then —
    A woman's eyes —
        And waves breaking —
            The way the wind blows —
    You will find it hard to remember
    Her lips —
            And the lamplight on the street-corner
    You who have known
    Flame of the sun's rising —
        Flight of swallows —
           A lover's nearness —
    For the soft rains of time will wash them away
    Siftings on siftings in oblivion —
    Till change has broken down and obliterated
    Even these sweet memories to the hard grey bones
    But the grey bones will not remember . . .

SECOND VOICE

    Man is but a fire breeding out of himself
    Ashes, a momentary incandescence

That gutters into death, a fatuous flame
Leaving nothing, for the ashes will not remember.

YOUTH

I fear the time of death and evening's strangeness
I, as the dead, will forget the place of my loves
There will be nothing remembered in that day
Only the mouldered smell of a dust that was mine.
What will remain? What will remain but the
Sun in that time; the wind then; and the moon's
Pale wanderings in those leaf-fallen nights
— The memory of a life once gladly lived...?
And shall there only then remain of me
A scent as of a grass a long time dead?

THE DEAD

Our lives were strange and noble; we believed
In the feel of the earth beneath us, trusted the sun
As it played on the leaves and flowers; and we conceived
Truth and true Beauty, End of things begun...
We, too, have laughed and sung our hundred songs
The sons we bore were perfect in our eyes
We hoped for them, but did not realize...
We saw them slain, — with faith we bore our wrongs
Watched we the clouds, and did not understand
We longed for happiness; we knew despair,
Lay, with our dreams, in the gutters; and were deceived
By eyes of women; whispered hand in hand,
And loved the moonlight on a lover's hair...
We were but a day in Eternity... still, we believed...

YOUTH

Believed in what?

THE DEAD

The Will of God.

YOUTH

How shall a man endure the Will of God and the
Days and the silence? In the years before him
Will he become as a ship that is lost at sea,
And drifting many ages in the deep
Can he believe in any Captain's skill,
The white gulls wheeling on the plight of him?

THE DEAD

We who are wise beyond your dreams of wisdom
Watched our "immortal" moments fade like grass —
Our visions deadened with the weight of years
We have gone forth beyond your bounds and borders
Our dwelling now is in Eternity
Where Time is shrivelled down to nothingness
We learnt our lesson in the day we died —
Life's not a game of money, banks, and houses,
No mere pretence that plays at love and mating
Of cheeks grown sunken and glad hair gone grey —
There *is* a subtler meaning in Existence
Who can but look on the stars and not believe?

YOUTH

It is hard to believe, not knowing, day to day
The first day's end, nor starting of the next,
Nor through dawn-mist to catch a glimpse of evening . . .
The tawny sands we tread in this short life
Washed in the surgings of Eternity
Can never hope to rise above their state
Of calm submission to the seas of Fate.

THE DEAD

There is a greater power than that of Fate
— The power of Love —
As red leaves follow where the wind has flown
So all men follow love when love is dead
And when the scent returns on the breath of the wind
Then in the faint scent of leaves at the year's ending
Come only the memories of the loves they bore . . .

YOUTH

Love? . . .

In the morn of my years there came a woman
A trembling upon the twilight of my life
Who came with the dawn of my time

as moonlight calling

As the moon calls to the tides she summons me —
This is the only Love that I have known
This brought me happiness;

In after years

I will remember this the love of my life
Cherishing the memory as no other —

FIRST VOICE

So you think that you are "in love" as you say?
But the years will show you how you were mistaken
You will recall perhaps the way her hair
Curled round her ears
But she will be a Sweet Memory as you will say
In the long after years of forgotten love.

THE DEAD

Frequently we have known the ecstatic agony

We too have known the abandonment of bliss
Sensing the heart through the lips that press
Coolly against one's own —

                    striving, across the pain
To send some feeling of the inward love . . .

SECOND VOICE

    That was long ago in the time of your living
    You thought that Love was all there was of pleasure
    But now they search the avaricious features
    Seeking a sign of the old remembered feeling
    But finding nothing left of the love that was there
    — Sixpence the price, it seems, for a change of passion
    Cupid astride a compact, — powder puff —
    Smoking a cigarette —

                 they are unable
    To pierce the crust of a cheap, unreal beauty
    To the Wealth of Love that lies, they're told, beneath.
    These are the lures of women, harlot-habits
    Who, half alive, invite to a fuller life
    And never loving would be loved by them
    For now the love of vanity persists
    Each striving to outdo the other's attractions
    Fantastic clothes (if any) entice and kindle
    The smouldering flame of desire in the other sex
    They try to stir to new affections hearts
    Already purged and drained of all their love
    Invoking a world of passion,

                 watch their years
    By the permutations of their frocks and fashions
    All designed to give the desired impression —
    Freshness of body that belies the soul.

THE DEAD
> But what of those who in proud and beautiful poems
> Have praised the beauty of women —

FIRST VOICE
> — Expecting Time
> To falter in his stride beholding them,
> Who call for a sudden hush in the ballroom of Life
> As each respective beauty sweeps the stair!

YOUTH
> I have read and heard read poetry —
> some of women
> Naming the grave mouth and the hair and eyes
> Praising the young stride and the sweep of garments —
> I too have tried to speak coherently
> Watching the smooth shoulders and the veiling hair
> To others the sound of these pen-whispered words
> Is madness —
> who have not seen the moving lips
> Nor felt the soothing quiet of a girl's breathing
> Knowing the hand's strain and the difficult labour
> In the effort to coax from the heart the stubborn words —

SECOND VOICE
> You think you are a poet, — preen yourself
> On the obscurest reveries of the inward gaze
> Lifting a wordy mirror of your affection
> To some poor common girl you made a goddess —

FIRST VOICE
> In the other days,
> the deep clear stars befriending,
> It was not hard to produce these lover's poems

Praising a woman's beauty with a pencil
Confident in the continuance of your living
Believing that you would meet with lips and hands
In some cool-scented paradise together
But now —
She who could never live without her lover
She who would never die without her charmer
Gone soon far from beyond the reach of hands
The unforgettable, unforgotten features
Soon lost within the emptiness of space.

THIRD VOICE

Yes, lost for ever
                              — for soon there will have come
A grinding discord in the tune of Life
Infinite things desired, lofty visions
All find their end with the coming of War
                                                          and instantly
A paradise is hurled to nothingness —

SECOND VOICE

And in the brutal holocaust of war
Swept by the lurid posters, roll of drums
His chapped hands fumbling rifle, hand grenade,
Each youth has time to contemplate his Soul
Feeling, perhaps, uneasy as his bullet
Pierces a stomach in the opposing trenches . . .
And there, where quietness is seldom known
While armies clash they move and feel the sun
As crushed plants take their respite gratefully
Whispering among them "The fair dead
Must all have known such moments, when the sun
Is warm and soothing to the frosted hand"

Enjoying the last glad wavering hours they know —
Soon all the lovable thoughts that moved from them
Swept from the mind of them in their departure —

THE DEAD

Where is the bravery of these youths in their dying?
Brought up to battle we took the offensive quickly
We kept our pride —
                    paid for it with our lives
We found the nadir we had shunned in dreams
Falling from the cliff among the shrieks of gulls
Reaching the crags below before we woke . . .

FIRST VOICE

These fought bravely for their country
Even some disbelieving
Some quick to battle
Some eager for adventure
Some from fear of weakness . . .
Died some "pro patria"
Walked bravely to hell for their country and traditions —
But now men have forgotten anger, and ambuscade —
The heated hand on the sword and the blood's rising
These have made killing their only business
Bored to an inch of extinction in the killing . . .

SECOND VOICE

Now is the time to flee while the danger is absent
The days of life forbid the ravelling of lengthy
Hopes;
        Night and the fabled Dead are near —

YOUTH

The still before the storm . . . I cannot wait for the

Crushing wave to swamp my happiness
The sky is ocean-deep and colourless
A ghastly still's in the air . . .
                              impending thunder
What if the storm should break and find us unready? . . .
This tells the ears what filters through my veins
The sense of doom . . .
                    this fatal clarity
Is sent to warn me of the destruction to follow —

THIRD VOICE
Men's fates are already set
There is no need of asking fortune-tellers
They will have brought this evil on themselves
For here are a million people surly with traffic
Each with his hereditary dower of instability
Each on his way to become a commercial corsair
Each with his fill of hollow aspirations
Competing with one another in the tawdry
Glitter and speed of machines, — mechanical mania —
Unable in the supervening blankness
Of middle age to sift the good from evil
Taking it all as one —
                    their only dread
Unpopularity and social inconsequence . . .
These need a cleansing, some all-purging tempest
To shake the stagnant pool of their convictions
Leaving with them fresh hopes as after a nightmare
For then the strange night-wonder will be upon them
These will stare as dream-awakened men in wonder
As in the Bardo the smug earth-passion dies
For now the moth-hour of their day is upon them —

FIRST VOICE

Yes and soon will come the cathartic energy
Which, skating on the slender ice of their life
These wrought themselves
                              in over-confidence
Trusting the thin weak crust of their melting traditions
To keep them from the icy depth below
But suddenly the ice will melt from under them
Plunging them into the vast abyss of War
Victims of their own self-germinated hell . . .

YOUTH

Then it seems that I am doomed to meet extinction
And all my loves and hates will die with me
No force is left to save me from this waste
This careful shaping of a life in vain
Which must, before it lives, find time to die!

THE DEAD

We who are gone where the grey winds call to you
— You, flesh-shrouded frame that bears the secret —
Beseech you not to leave it undiscovered
A short time hence you will be dead as we are
And the secret, hardly known, will die with you
Returning useless with your dust to rot
Returning as a taunt to all the dead
Reminding us of our own great failure, who
Have lived and died
                            — and left the truth unfound
For after death it is too late to discover
The secret that the living must unveil —

You cannot dig men's hearts up from the dust
And think to tell their secrets from their bones
You cannot stare between their eyepits thinking
To solve the riddle of Eternity
For when you are dead you will become as we are
Rising again but formless in the rising
Intangible fluids that were once alive
Who once had trod the avenue of Life
As you do now —
                              we strove in vain to find
The secret of our living
                              for without it
Each buried dust and mouldered skeleton
Finds in the grave fit mould, fit place of rot.

Now I have heard the voices of the dead
I have read out the writing on the wall
And wearied out my brain upon the secret
And torn my mind against the jagged dark
And still I find no answer to it all!

CHORUS
All that is asked of you is Trust and Hope
Without these Man is as some animal
That gropes in sea-pools with its tentacles
That reaches up and out for Truth beneath
The slow green surgings of the underwave
Until abandonment of self to God
Brings hope into the algae of the soul.
Here is the secret of your time of living
Given to you to find before your dying

Without it you can never find that faith
Which all must have before they come to their God.

YOUTH

What hope is there that I shall *live* again?
— For Life bore in, soon it must bear away
Can I, a wretched puppet of a man
With death before him struggle to improve
This hollow shell within himself —

this soul

This fabrication built of Autumn roses
Which soon must wither on the ground?

— What is

Religion but an anodyne to Life?

CHORUS

Above the bones and the grave
Motionless, placed for ever
Motionless, even in Time
Safeguard of Grief
Defence of Despair
There stands the Highest Paragon of Men
Whom some call Love or Truth —

and others God;

And from that Fount of Sense Untellable
There springs the Source of Life and Happiness
A cool Oasis in the Desert of Life
Where all that lives spreads out from the hands of God
In wider circles through the Lake of Night
In which His hand has dropped the stone of Life.

YOUTH

Can He give me dawnlight at evening? Can the
Twilight of my hopes be turned to morning?

Can He let form within my hands once more
The present, cradled as a glass of wine
Before it drains to a modest nothingness?
Great minds have sought Him
                              — lacking someone else
He has been second always. Pitiful?
— A God who's always taken second place
That might prove useful and yet never proves
That never fits a corner or shows use —

CHORUS

Did you forget so soon, O faithless man,
How in the time of winter's frost and snow
One coming
                    gave His life that you might live
And saved the soul of you?
                                        He came with kindness
With freedom on his lips,
                                  but, scorning, you
Believed Him not —
                          Whose words you might have learned
But now must read unseen —
                                    Can you not hear
A Gentle Voice that sounded down the Ages
Coming a long way off as over water:-
"I am the Way, the Truth, the Light;
                                          no man
Cometh unto the Father but by Me"?

YOUTH

At last I see! The whirling tissue of thought
Grows firm beneath me —
                              now can be seen the motive

That led the saints down their forbidden roads
Who leaped the toothed and cragged crevasse of Death
At their Ordainer's word
        ignoring Time
Whom they left to hone and whet his blade alone.
What faith is this, that trusts when hope is dead!
What hope is this, that hopes when faith has flown!
Their eyes are as those of a maid to her lover. These
Questing and passive bore His news to their brothers
Who had no thought for themselves in the face of danger . . .
Now that these haunting fears have gone their way
— Importunate talons that clutch my heart in vain —
I am glad of a life no longer fugitive,
Glad of the accident of being alive!

CHORUS

Give you His glories their longevity
Brave you the strange vicissitudes of Time
And thank Him for the abandon of His giving
Cease doubting what is shadow, what is flesh
What matters it to you except that God
Has pierced your stubborn heart, — and come alive?

. . . .

The following two poems were written by John Magee between the ages of 14 and 17 when he was a pupil at Rugby.

I stood alone
And stared into a starlit sky,
Hearing only the hum
Of distant worlds, whirling
Silently through space; and suddenly
I knew! Adumbral Truth
Took shape before my eyes, appearing
Out of nothingness,
Glimmering through a world of dark,
Chimeric fancy. Its voice
Re-echoed down the ages, wave
Upon wave of swelling sound,
Until the stars
In their gigantic unison
Took up the strain, and all the sky
Was filled with a deep,
Pellucid chorus ... then it ceased,
And all the thrill of revelation
Sank into the obscurity of
Reason ...
And I gazed up into the
Cold, hard faces of the stars.

This is a monstrous night!
It presses in my ears, my eyes,
As if to crush out
My very soul. I hear no sound
Except the urgent
Ticking of a clock, and some busy whisper
Of the wind. Above, the stars
Have hid their faces from my eyes. The aspen moon
Slips silently behind a cloud
As if afraid to shine; and somewhere in this thick,
Unfathomable gloom, there is
Reality.
Its shape, its form, its depth
I can not know; incomprehensible,
A feeling, not a thing; but this I know:
A hand stretched out to mine. I heard a Voice
Whispering a secret to my soul . . .

*The next three poems were recently discovered by the
Magee family. They are published here for the first time.*

ENTRY OF THE HEROES

(being a satire provoked by Sunday Chapel at Rugby)

But who are these who enter one by one
The darkened halls, their passive labours done?
— Who these black minions, — though with Youth endowed,
Who file within, a pale plebeian crowd?
Are these the servants of a loftier race?
And why this torpid stare on every face?
The silent, awestruck throng grows thick, until
The waking buildings soon begin to fill
With shadowy, stooping forms; they take their place
In ordered rows, a sombre populace.
Now all is silent, and a breathless hush
Awaits the advent throng; a golden flush
Illumes the portal designate; all eyes
Embrace the door to obviate surprise …

The organ-trump sends up a regal note;
"The Heroes come!" — the cry in every throat
Unspoken. Then, in glory unsurpassed
They enter, each more splendid than the last.
To lead the throng comes Paris, aged lord,
In sisters rich, but hesitant of word.

Achilles next — he struts with kingly gait;
His crested plumelets nod, importunate,
As if to ape his motions, he whose trade
Consists of voicing endless, dull, tirade;
What care is this we see upon his brow,
— Or has this frown become ingrained now?
Him do his fawning sycophants beguile,
For seldom do they see Achilles smile.
Then Memnon comes, in volume infinite,
For Law and Order caring not a whit;
Among these minions sits his only son,
But who, from out the swart, may find the one?
Next Ajax, of the bright proboscid pink,
Ascribed by some to choler, some to drink;
A vermeil cape refulgent on his back,
To toilers kind — a terror to the slack.
Then wide-eyed Jason, sunken at the cheek,
His unctuous locks brushed smooth, his gaze oblique.
But whose this hirsute countenance severe,
— A second Esau, horrent at the ear?
Then comes Apollo, scholar laureate;
In accent strange — in figure — adequate,
With Mars, his truckling in the same pursuit
(though epidermically destitute.)
Then Perseus comes, in lucent robes bedight,
Of martial fame, subordinate in height.
He leads the Arm of Youth to victory,
— His air more apt than his ability.
And last of all Orion, he whose ear
Has suffered from a pugilist career.

THE FOREST

Midnight —
How still is the world tonight!
A forest lies ahead, sunk in slumber;
From its shadowy depths
No voice
Calls to welcome me. Must I step
From the soft moon's silvered light
Into eternal night?

I entered.
At once I was aware of light, and yet
No sound I heard. Something
Brushed my face. My straining ears
Caught nothing. As I walked
I seemed to move further
And further
From Life. Death
Beckoned, drawing me ever onward
Into its gaping bosom;
The trees
Mocked me; faces gnarled and lichened
Leered derision, pointing their long, thin fingers
Towards the End;
The End … and then?
I stopped. Deep silence
Filled my ears, my nose, my throat,
Choking me …
I felt my brow; my eyes
Were filled with sweat. I turned
And, turning, ran, stumbling blindly

Through the forest. Fear
Was at my heels.
I had no eyes for leering trees
And pointing fingers. My knees
Began to sag, and I could see no light.
Fear, life's greatest Hustler, drove me on.
I fought for breath. I tried to shout.
No answer met my troubled call
But that of Echo — still I could see no light.
Fainting, I prayed:-
Oh God! ... and then
I saw the moon. I ran ...

I stopped, and raised my head.
The moon smiled down at me. I looked
At the forest, peaceful now,
And wondered at my foolishness.

(Rugby, 1937)

OH ONCE AGAIN

To climb aloft and watch the dawn ascend
Earth's haze-enshrouded rim. To dally high
And see the morning ghosts forsake their blend
For sundry silhouettes. To catch the sky
Transformed, its fawn and silv'ry tints now rife
With brilliant hues recast. To ease my craft
Below as golden darts give birth to life
And set the world astir. To catch a shaft
Of beaming warmth, and quickened by its touch
Assault its course through hills of airy fleece.
To burst at last above the crests and clutch
The fleeting freedom — endless blue, at peace.

1941